THE ART OF DRAWING™

Manga Pets

by
david antram

A⁺
Smart Apple Media

Published by Smart Apple Media,
an imprint of Black Rabbit Books
P.O. Box 3263, Mankato, Minnesota 56002
www.blackrabbitbooks.com

Published by arrangement with
The Salariya Book Company Ltd

Cataloging-in-Publication Data is available
from the Library of Congress

Printed in the United States
At Corporate Graphics,
North Mankato, Minnesota

9 8 7 6 5 4 3 2 1

ISBN: 978-1-62588-353-7

contents

making a start

The key to drawing well is learning to look carefully. Study your subject until you know it really well. Keep a sketchbook with you and draw whenever you get the chance. Even doodling is good—it helps to make your drawing more confident. You'll soon develop your own style of drawing, but this book will help you to find your way.

Practice drawing basic head and body shapes...

...then try adding facial detail.

quick sketches

Try sketching your own pets (or friends' pets) in different positions.

Look at the way light reflects in eyes and practice drawing it.

perspective

Perspective is a way of drawing objects so that they look as though they have three dimensions. Note how the part that is closest to you looks larger, and the part furthest away from you looks smaller. That's just how things look in real life.

The vanishing point (V.P.) is the place in a perspective drawing where parallel lines appear to meet. The position of the vanishing point depends on the viewer's eye level.

V.P.

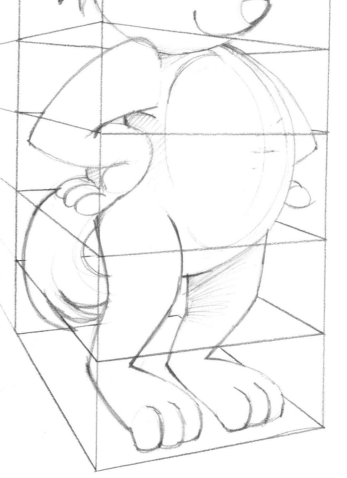

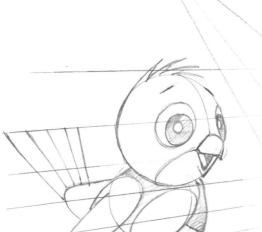

6

two-point perspective drawing

Two-point perspective uses two vanishing points: one for lines running along the length of the subject, and one on the opposite side for lines running across the width of the subject.

Low eye level
(view from below)

V.P.

V.P.

In this drawing the vanishing points are low down. This gives the impression that you are looking up at the subject—very dramatic!

V.P.

V.P.

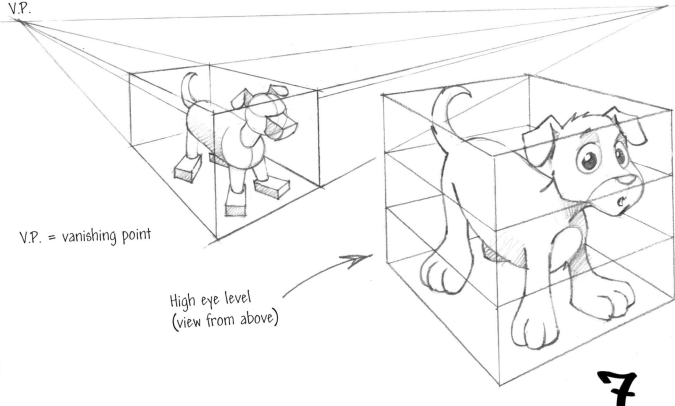

V.P. = vanishing point

High eye level
(view from above)

7

materials

Remember, the best equipment and materials will not necessarily make the best drawing—only practice will.

pencils

Try out different grades of pencils. Hard pencils make fine gray lines and soft pencils make softer, darker marks.

erasers

are useful for cleaning up drawings and removing construction lines.

paper

Bristol paper is good for crayons, pastels, and felt-tip pens. Watercolor paper is thicker; it is the best choice for water-based paints or inks.

Use this sandpaper block if you want to shape your pencil to a really sharp point.

8

inks

Use colored inks straight from the bottle or dilute them with water.

felt-tip pens

Felt-tip pens usually come in sets of mixed colors. The ones that make very thin lines are called fineliners.

Ink

Mixing palette

Fineliners

Dip-in pen nibs

Brushes

Correction fluid

Gouache

pens

Technical drawing pens have cartridges which can be refilled or replaced. Old-fashioned dip-in pens are much cheaper and come in many different styles and sizes.

Watercolors

paints

Ordinary watercolors are translucent (see-through); gouache is not. Try other kinds of paints, too.

Technical drawing pens

9

styles

Try different types of drawing papers and materials. Experiment with pens, from felt-tips to ballpoints, and make interesting marks. What happens if you draw with pen and ink on wet paper?

Ink silhouette

Silhouette is a style of drawing which mainly relies on solid dark shapes.

Felt-tips come in a range of line widths. The wider pens are good for filling in large areas of flat tone.

Pencil drawings can include a vast amount of detail and tone. Try different grades of pencil to get a range of light and shade effects in your drawings.

Hatching   Cross-hatching

Lines drawn in **ink** cannot be erased, so unless you are very confident you may want to sketch your drawing in pencil first.

It can be tricky adding light and shade to a drawing with a pen. Use a solid layer of ink for the very darkest areas and cross-hatching (straight lines criss-crossing each other) for ordinary dark tones. Use hatching (straight lines running parallel to each other) for midtones.

11

body proportions

Heads in manga are drawn slightly bigger than in real life. Legs and body make up more than half the overall height of the character.

Use columns to proportion head and body size. For a four-legged creature like this, use two columns.

The eye level is about midway down the head.

Use points to identify joints such as knees and elbows, so when you add detail to your character these will be in proportion.

inking

Refillable inking pens come in various tip sizes. The tip is what determines the width of the line that is drawn. Sizes include: 0.1, 0.5, 1.0, 2.0 mm.

Here's one way of inking over your final pencil drawing.

Different tones of ink can be used to add depth to the drawing.
Mix ink with water to achieve the tones you need.

Correction fluid usually comes in small bottles or in pen format. This can be useful for cleaning up ink lines.

13

heads

Manga heads have a distinctive style and shape. Drawing different facial expressions is very important—it shows instantly what your character is thinking or feeling.

1. Start by drawing the head shape. Think wider oval shapes for cat's faces, circular shapes for mice, and longer shapes for horses or squirrels.

2. Draw two construction lines along the center of your shape. Next, draw one down the middle. These will position the eyes.

3. Use the space created by the construction lines to center the nose and mouth.

4. Add a pupil to the eye and draw in the nose, mouth, and ears.

5. Add more detail such as eyes, eyebrows, and teeth.

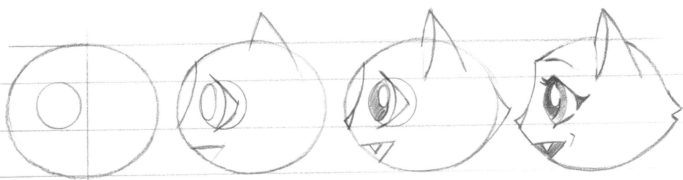

Practice drawing heads from different angles and with different facial expressions.

Centerline

Excited

Frightened

Dreamy

Mean

Happy

Worried

Whichever way the head is turned, the nose and mouth always stay on the centerline.

15

chibifying

C hibi is a manga style where the subject is small and cute. Any drawing can be made into chibi style by exaggerating features while keeping the body small.

This is an example of how to draw in a traditional non-manga style. Note the traditional body and facial proportions, and the lifelike quality of the drawing.

Try drawing from life (or pictures) to get an understanding of how muscles look and how arms and legs bend so you know where to draw lines.

These are examples of manga style. Note the construction circles are smaller and rounder, producing a smaller shape, the facial features are more cartoonish and some of the features are enlarged, such as the ears and feet.

Your manga pets can come in all shapes and sizes. You can change the construction circles and lines depending on the type of animal, or what kind of character you want it to be.

akemi

This boy is having fun, circled by his winged pet Akemi who protects him at all times.

1. Draw ovals for the head, body, and hips. Add center lines to divide the head vertically and horizontally. These will help you to place the ears and the nose.

2. Add lines for the spine and the angle of the hips and shoulders.

Cat's ears

3. Draw stick arms and legs, with dots where the joints are. Add outline shapes for hands and feet.

4. Sketch the cat in the same way—add a spiky effect to create a bushy tail.

5. Using the construction lines as a guide, start to build up the main shapes and features.

These little circles are to remind you where the elbows and knees go.

6. Draw the clothes, hair, and facial features. This is where your drawing really starts to come to life.

Try a feathered wing effect. Forward-pointing paws create a streamlined image.

Why not add a catlike sound effect?

meow

Shadow

Drawing movement lines (in this case, swimming) creates the impression of speed.

7. If you don't want your construction lines to show, erase them before you do the final shading and details.

8. Now finish all the little details such as the shading on the hair and clothes, and the cat's fur. Don't rush! The more carefully you do these finishing touches, the better your drawing will look. Try finishing your drawing off in ink.

kazuki dog

Kazuki is very loyal, full of energy, and always wanting to play. Draw him running as he's always in action!

1. Draw a circle for the head and ovals for the body and hips.

2. Add lines for the spine and the angle of the hips and shoulders.

3. Draw stick arms and legs with dots for the joints.

4. Use your guidelines to sketch in the neck and facial features.

5. Using the construction lines as a guide, start drawing in the main shapes of the body.

Think about the angle of a dog's legs—when they are running fast, they bend at a sharp angle and bring their back legs up high.

Small circles indicate the positions of elbows and knees.

6. Now start to sketch out the final shapes of ears, feet, and tail.

Remember perspective! His back feet look bigger because they are closest to us.

Tongue sticking out

Folds in the skin

You can experiment with different tails. A bushy tail can show the dog is moving fast.

woof

7. If you don't want your construction lines to show, erase them carefully before you add the finishing touches: shading, facial features, and the patches in the fur.

21

satsuki

2atsuki's sassy, sly, and always around when something goes wrong, but she gets away with it for being so adorable.

1. Draw circles for the head and the body—don't forget your center line.

2. Add a line for the spine and half-circles on either side for the legs.

3. Draw stick arms and circles for hands.

4. Using your construction lines, add the shape of the head, legs, feet, and paws.

5. Flesh out the arms and legs, adding details to the ears and tail. Try some basic facial features.

Practice sassy facial expressions

Add the shape of the tail.

6. Draw the pattern of the fur, the positions of the paws, and embellish the face.

Think about color: a white patch on the face will show more detail. A white patch on the stomach will show off the body shape.

Create fur by drawing jagged lines instead of solid lines around the basic body shape.

One tooth!

7. Erase your construction lines if you don't want them to show.

8. Take plenty of time to finish the details of the face and body, shading where the light won't reach.

eyes

Draw the eye shape and then add the pupil.

Either leave the highlights white, or paint them white using gouache or correcting fluid.

Highlight

23

maru monkey

Maru is a very curious creature and loves being around people. He enjoys exploring and discovering new things.

2. Add a line for the spine and others to show the angle of the hips and shoulders.

3. Draw stick arms and legs with dots for the joints and outline shapes for the hands and feet. Draw a line for the position of the tail.

I. Draw different-sized ovals for the head, body, and hips.

4. Using your construction lines as a guide, draw the main shapes of the body and position the facial features.

Ears are positioned with the center line in the middle.

Circles show positions of elbows and knees.

Curly tail

5. Add more detail to the face shape-a heart-shaped face will show off his eyes. Flesh out the arms, legs, body, and tail and add some fur.

Practice curious facial expressions.

6. Erase the construction lines if you want to and finish off all the remaining details. Try using a highlight in maru's eyes.

You could try finishing this drawing in ink.

The position of the thumb is important.

Think about the feet. A chimp will have feet more proportioned to a human than other animals.

There are different ways of drawing fur. A more exaggerated effect could show that an animal is wilder than a more domesticated pet.

25

daiki donkey

This donkey can always be relied upon to make a lot of noise. He can't be trusted with any secrets!

1. Draw different-sized circles for the hips, body, and mouth. This time we need a second smaller circle for the donkey's elongated head shape.

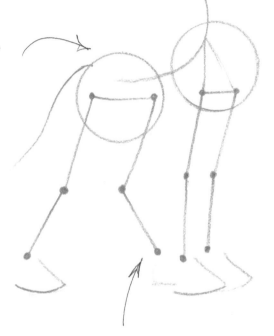

2. Draw in a curved line connecting the circles, for the spine and neck.

Eyes and ears always go on the center line. Sketch an open mouth shape and use this to connect the two head circles.

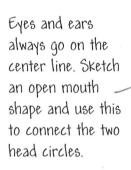

3. Draw stick legs with dots for the joints. The back legs should be open.

Circles show positions of the joints.

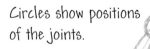

Think about the feet—hooves are triangular-shaped.

4. Using your construction lines, sketch in the basic shapes of the head, body, legs, and tail.

5. Erase construction lines and take your time to finish all the details.

Look at the nostrils and mouth detail!

Bushy mane

eee ore

Why not try finishing this drawing in ink?

Animals like this have muscular bodies. Look at pictures of donkeys or horses and study the way their muscles look so you know where to add lines. Also look at the shape of their knees.

27

kenzo frog

Kenzo is not the sharpest tool in the shed, but he has good intentions and makes everyone around him laugh.

Remember to draw where joints should be.

1. Draw the various ovals and construction lines. This time we need two overlapping circles sitting on the center line for the eyes.

A triangle at the base of the head makes the bottom part of the mouth.

2. Add the limbs, feet, and hands. Create an open mouth shape by drawing a curved line from the center line of the head, and another from the center line of the closest eye. Connect them.

28

3. Start drawing the details, such as the webbed feet and eyes. Flesh out the body shape. Look at the typical body shape of a frog; the front and back legs are long and flexible.

Long fingers

Large pupils

4. Erase construction lines before adding final details such as shading and the highlights in the eyes.

Shading: think about the areas the light doesn't reach, like the insides of his legs.

5. Here's the same drawing finished with brush and ink. This style is often used for illustrations in fashion magazines. Decide which lines you want to ink in before you make any brushmarks.

MIU

Miu is a good luck charm. Her owner keeps her on his shoulder, and Miu protects him from harm.

1. Draw the basic ovals and construction lines. The hamster's body shape is very round, so draw circles for the legs too.

2. Use your construction lines to add facial features and ears. Draw the arms as large folds, with long flat paws and feet.

Try sketching from a different angle:

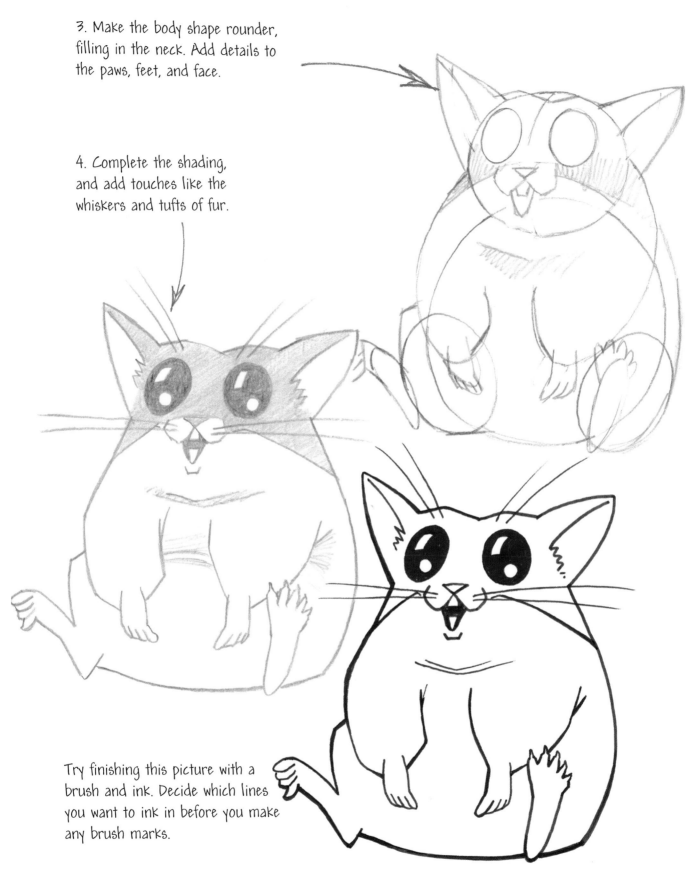

3. Make the body shape rounder, filling in the neck. Add details to the paws, feet, and face.

4. Complete the shading, and add touches like the whiskers and tufts of fur.

Try finishing this picture with a brush and ink. Decide which lines you want to ink in before you make any brush marks.

31

glossary

Composition The positioning of the various parts of a picture on the drawing paper.

Construction lines Guidelines used in the early stages of a drawing which are usually erased later.

Cross-hatching A series of criss-crossing lines used to add shade to a drawing.

Hatching A series of parallel lines used to add shade to a drawing.

Manga A Japanese word for "comic" or "cartoon"; also the style of drawing that is used in Japanese comics.

Neko The Japanese word for "cat"; also a manga character that is part-human, part-cat.

Silhouette A drawing that shows only a dark shape, like a shadow, sometimes with a few details left white.

Three-dimensional Having an effect of depth, so as to look like a real character rather than a flat picture.

Tone The contrast between light and shade that helps to add depth to a picture.

Vanishing point The place in a perspective drawing where parallel lines appear to meet.

index